Getting to Know Special Ed:

The General Educator's Essential Guide

By Gerry Klor

Publications

LRP Publications
Horsham, Pennsylvania 19044

Library of Congress Cataloging-in-Publication Data

Klor, Gerry.
    Getting to know special ed : the general educator's essential guide / by Gerry Klor.
    p. cm.
    ISBN 1-57834-039-X
    1. Special education--Handbooks, manuals, etc. 2. Children with disabilities--Education--Handbooks, manuals, etc. I. Title.

LC3965.K59 2005
371.9--dc22

2003070233

About the Author

GERRY KLOR worked in special education for more than 30 years as a school psychologist and director of special education. *Getting to Know Special Ed: The General Educator's Essential Guide* is based upon his experience of training and consulting general education staff to work with special education students. In addition to his work in public schools, he was on the graduate department faculty of Dominican University of California and San Francisco State University. Klor is also author of *Say the Right Thing: A Guide to Responding to Parents' IEP Requests* and *What Every Parent Needs to Know about Special Education*, both published by LRP Publications. His firm, Educational & Psychological Solutions, provides consultation and training in the area of special education. He can be reached at *glklor@aol.com*.

Table of Contents

About This Book

Written for General Educators

For many general educators, special education processes and procedures are complicated and hard to understand. Often the documents that describe the legal and procedural requirements are dense and filled with technical language. *Getting to Know Special Ed: The General Educator's Essential Guide* is written specifically for general education staff and clearly and simply describes everything you need to know to meet your responsibilities under the Individuals with Disabilities Education Act.

Explains Procedures & Processes

This book is designed to take you through the special education process, from referral to development of the individualized educational plan, or IEP. It provides guidance on how to handle your responsibilities to special education students enrolled in your classes. Not sure how discipline is handled for a special education student or what to do about accommodations and modifications? You can find the information you need right here.

Concrete & Specific

Getting to Know Special Ed: The General Educator's Essential Guide offers specific suggestions and concrete examples to help you meet your legal responsibilities to special education students enrolled in your classes. This book provides practical, easy-to-implement classroom strategies to assist you in your work with special education students.

A Word of Caution

The information and guidance presented in this book are based upon the author's experience in the field and his understanding of current special education law and regulation. *Getting to Know Special*

Ed: The General Educator's Essential Guide was written to help you understand special education, but it is not intended to replace the guidance of your local special education director or the advice of the school district's attorney.

A Final Note: 'General' vs. 'Regular'

The author uses the terms "general educator" and "general education" rather than "regular educator" and "regular education" to avoid the inference that anything other than regular in this context would be irregular. However, the word "regular" may appear where it simply makes more sense.

Chapter 1

Why You Need to Know about Special Education

The Short Answer

The Individuals with Disabilities Education Act, known as IDEA, is a federal statute that describes the legally required procedures to educate students with disabilities in public schools. All general educators, as a condition of their employment in a public school system, are obligated to obey all laws and regulations governing the education of students in their care. Accordingly, all general educators are required to participate in the education of students with disabilities as described by IDEA.

IDEA '97 Expanded the General Educators' Responsibilities

When Congress reauthorized the Individual with Disabilities Education Act in 1997, it expanded general educators' responsibilities to participate in the education of students with disabilities to reflect the federal government's belief that such students should, to the maximum extent possible, participate in the general education curriculum. To ensure that students with disabilities were able to access general education classes, it was necessary to mandate greater general educator participation in the special education process. Prior to IDEA '97, general education staff were required to participate in the referral of students with suspected disabilities for special education evaluation and to provide accommodations and modifications for those students enrolled in their general education classes. Under IDEA '97, general education teachers are mandatory members of the individualized education program (IEP) team for all special education students, including students being considered for special education who are participating in or may participate in their general education classes. In addition, general education teachers must be involved in the development of the IEP, specifically to describe any supplementary aids or supports necessary for the student to participate and progress in the general curriculum. As part of the IEP team, general educators are expected to be knowledgeable regarding the contents of the IEP and responsible for implementing any specific activities assigned to them, such as following behavior intervention plans or making adjustments regarding testing and grading.

Special Education Enters the Mainstream

Many years ago students with moderate and severe disabilities were educated in a separate system of public education, often attending classes on segregated sites or centers, while students with mild disabilities were served on regular school campuses. More recently, when these students with more severe disabilities attended school along with general education students, their opportunities for contact were limited and their educational needs were handled separately. In 1997, the IDEA changed how students with more significant disabilities were educated, moving them from the margins into the mainstream. In essence, where the original IDEA mandated access to the local school building, the 1997 amendments provided greater access to the general education classroom and curriculum. It was inevitable that this change in how special education students were to be taught would have significant implications for the general education staff.

IDEA Increased Special Education Students' Participation in General Education

As more students with disabilities attended special education classes located on general education campuses, it created a greater opportunity for interaction between disabled and nondisabled students. Initially, students with moderate to severe disabilities were integrated into daily campus activities, such as recess and lunch. Gradually, some of these students were integrated into general classes, but their participation in the curriculum was limited. By the time IDEA '97 came along, many disabled students were expected to participate to some degree in the general education curriculum, and general education teachers were required to play a significant role in the education of special education students.

IDEA Increased General Educator's Legal and Liability Exposure

As more students with moderate to severe disabilities participated in regular classes and the general education curriculum, general educators were drawn into legal disputes involving special education students placed in their classrooms. When general education participation is required for development and implementation of an IEP, it becomes part of that disabled student's entitlement to education. Accordingly, when there is a dispute regarding whether or not a student with a disability has received his legal entitlement to a "free, appropriate public education," commonly referred to as FAPE, the general education staff may become involved in a variety of legal proceedings. In fact, there are many cases where the special education student's participation in general education becomes the crucial issue in determining if the IEP has been implemented properly and if the student has received FAPE. In some situations, if the general educator refuses to comply with the special education student's IEP, she not only exposes the school district to serious legal and financial consequences, but she could be subjected to disciplinary action and sued, as an individual, for money damages.

General Educators Need to Know about Special Education

Because you are considered to be an integral part of the public school educational services available to students with disabilities, it is vital that you understand and accept your responsibilities as outlined by IDEA. Not only is it important for you to be knowledgeable about special education procedures in general, but you must be aware of any portions of a special education student's IEP that require specific action on your part. If you are familiar with the contents of your students' IEPs and implement all portions that apply to general education, you will meet your responsibilities under IDEA and protect yourself and your school district from a legal challenge that could have significant fiscal consequences.

Chapter 2

What Are My Legal Responsibilities for 'Child Find'?

The Short Answer

The IDEA requires that every state have a process for locating, identifying and evaluating all children with disabilities who are in need of special education and related services. The process is referred to as "child find" and general educators play an important role in referring students with suspected disabilities for special education evaluation. (34 CFR 300.125)

Students with Disabilities in Elementary Schools

The majority of students with disabilities will enter school at kindergarten along with their nondisabled peers as general education students. At some point in their school careers, a general education teacher observes that they are not developing at the same rate as other students in the classroom. A student may have difficulty gaining academic skills, demonstrate atypical behavior, or is not responding appropriately to instruction, among other indicators that an evaluation may be necessary. Regardless of the specific problem that draws the teacher's attention, it is clear that the student is failing to make progress when compared to peers, so the student may have a suspected disability. Under the IDEA, as a general education teacher, you are expected to refer for assessment any student who appears to have a suspected disability to determine if the student is disabled and requires special education programs and services.

Child Find at Secondary Schools

Most students with disabilities will be identified during their elementary-school years or earlier, but some students' needs for special education may not become apparent until they enter middle school or, in some cases, high school. At the secondary level, in addition to general education teachers, grade-level counselors and administrators are expected to participate in child find. Counselors should monitor students who are failing classes to determine if the reason for the lack of academic success could be attributed to a suspected disability. Similarly, administrators who are involved in student discipline should be aware of students whose persistent misbehaviors may be signs of a suspected disability. Because secondary schools are more demanding academically and require more sophisticated interpersonal skills, students with disabilities have greater difficulty in these environments, and their underlying disabilities may be masked by behavior problems and a defensive attitude. General educators working at the secondary level need to be aware of the possibility that a student who is having behavior problems and demonstrating a defiant attitude may be a student with a disability who is unable to cope with the demands of the secondary-school setting. Although fewer students with disabilities are identified in middle school and high school, all general educators in these settings are expected to be looking for students with suspected disabilities.

General Educators Should Review Students Who Are Failing

Under IDEA, you share in the responsibility to locate students who may have suspected disabilities and may need special education programs and services. You are in a unique position to assist in the identification of potential special education students because you serve all students and are able to discriminate between students who are making satisfactory progress and those who are failing. If you systematically review students who are failing and consider if they may have a suspected disability, you are meeting your IDEA responsibilities under child find.

General Educators Should Refer Promptly

There have been many legal cases in which the school district's general educators did not exercise their child find responsibilities. In these cases, the educators did not promptly identify the students' possible disabilities and, as a result, the students did not receive timely services. Tragically, some students are not appropriately identified until their high school years and do not receive special education programs and services during most of their school careers. When these cases are reviewed, the records reflect that there was ample evidence the student was having difficulty for many years, but the general educators didn't refer the student for assessment. There are often reasons why these students weren't referred for special education consideration, including situational factors such as divorces, deaths and frequent moves from school to school. Regardless of any mitigating circumstances, the courts have held that general educators must be proactive in identifying students who may have a suspected disability and should promptly refer such students for assessment.

School Districts Must Train General Educators

General education staff must be provided with training to be able to correctly implement their school district's "child find" activities. When general educators are hired, they need to be trained in the specific procedures the school district employs to identify students with suspected disabilities. In addition, school districts should offer training on a periodic basis to ensure all general educators are familiar with their legal responsibilities under IDEA to locate, identify and serve students with disabilities.

Chapter 3

How Does the Referral Process Work?

The Short Answer

Under IDEA, each school district must adopt procedures to locate, identify and evaluate all students with suspected disabilities in order to provide special education programs and services to students who are eligible. Parents, school district personnel and other interested parties can make referrals for special education assessment.

Districts Must Inform Parents

School districts are required to provide to the parents of school-age children information that will enable them to refer their students for special education consideration. School districts typically provide parents with copies of all legally required district policies and procedures, including the special education referral process, when they complete the paperwork to enroll their child in school. In some cases, school districts will publish the special education referral process and annually send a copy to the parent of every student. Regardless of the method, school districts must demonstrate that they have taken steps to inform parents of the procedure used to refer a child for special education consideration. (34 CFR 300.129, 34 CFR 300.320, 34 CFR 300.500-529)

Districts Must Train General Educators

The district's special education referral process requires that staff members be trained in the procedures to be followed when a student is referred for special education consideration. In addition to understanding their responsibilities to locate and identify students with suspected disabilities, general education staff members also must be familiar with how to assist parents who are interested in referring their child for special education consideration.

The Referral Process Is a Legal Requirement

The special education referral procedures outlined in the IDEA are legal requirements, and school districts must be able to demonstrate that they have followed the appropriate steps within the required time sequence, if there is a challenge. Accordingly, school districts must be able to document, in writing, what they did and when they did it. Should the school district not be able to demonstrate that it has followed the correct procedure within the required timelines by furnishing written documentation, they cannot prevail in a special education legal proceeding and are out of compliance with the requirements of the IDEA. As a result, the special education referral process requires a paper trail to verify that the appropriate steps are followed in a timely manner. (34 CFR 300.320, 34 CFR 300.500-529)

Procedures for Parent Referrals

There are many reasons why parents will refer their child for special education consideration. Some parents may have their child assessed outside the school district, and the assessment indicates their child may have a disability. Other parents may inform the school or district that they are concerned their child is not progressing adequately. Regardless of the reason, parents are able to refer their children for assessment to determine if the child has a disability that requires a special education program or service.

When parents refer their child for special education consideration, the school district must inform the parent of the appropriate steps and time lines that are legally required.

- The parents will be asked to put their request for assessment in writing, so it is documented.

- Once the school district receives the parents' request, the district sends the parents a letter that confirms receipt of the referral and indicates the district has <u>15 calendar days</u> to determine if it will conduct the assessment.

- To establish if there is evidence of a suspected disability, the district may request a meeting with the student's parents and teacher or ask for referral information forms to be completed.

- Once the district has reviewed the referral information, it must notify the parents, in writing, within 15 days that it intends to evaluate the student or that it will not evaluate the student because it has determined there is no evidence of a suspected disability.

- If the district decides not to evaluate a student referred for special education consideration, it must send a letter that documents the reasons for the decision, informs the parents of their right to appeal that decision, and provides the parents with a copy of the district's Parent Rights & Procedural Safeguards.

- If the district decides there is evidence of suspected disability, it will inform the parents, in writing, and send them an assessment plan that describes the proposed evaluation.

- If the parents agree to the assessment plan, they will sign it and return it to the district.

- Once the district receives the signed assessment plan, they must complete the evaluation and present the information to the parents at an individualized education program (IEP) meeting within 50 calendar days. (34 CFR 300.320, 34 CFR 300.500-529, 34 CFR 300.530-536, 34 CFR 300.340-350)

Procedures for Staff Referrals

You and other general education staff members are key players in the school districts' efforts to locate and identify students with suspected disabilities. Teachers, administrators and other instructional staff members should be familiar with the process and procedures the school district uses to refer students for special education consideration. If a staff member believes that a student may have a suspected disability, she should notify the school administration and complete the district's special education referral form. At this point, many school districts schedule a conference with the student's parent(s), teacher and administrator to discuss the referral and document any accommodations and/or modifications that have been made prior to referring the student for special education consideration. At the meeting, it may be decided to move ahead with an assessment and complete the appropriate paperwork. If the parent agrees to an evaluation, the district will complete the assessment and present the findings to the parent within 50 days from the date it received the signed assessment permission. (34 CFR 300.320, 34 CFR 300.500-529, 34 CFR 300.530-536, 34 CFR 300.340-350)

Chapter 4

Which Students Should I Refer to Special Education?

The Short Answer

You are responsible for referring students with suspected disabilities for assessment to determine if they have a disability that requires a special education program and/or service. Students who should be considered for referral may demonstrate a broad range of suspected disabilities, including impairments in cognitive, academic, social, emotional, language, motor, or visual abilities that adversely affect their education. (34 CFR 300.7, 34 CFR 300.125)

Students Who Should Not Be Referred

In any given classroom, there are a number of students who may not be making satisfactory progress. Of the students who are having difficulty, some may have suspected disabilities and others may not. In reviewing the students who are not performing, it is useful to set aside those who are excluded from special education eligibility by the IDEA. According to the IDEA, students who lack instruction in reading or math or are limited English proficient should not be referred for special education consideration. The reason for these specific exclusions is to recognize that if a student has not had the opportunity to learn because she has not been in school before, she should not be considered disabled simply because she has not been taught. Likewise, a student who does not speak English may not be considered a student with a suspected disability simply because of a lack of English proficiency. In addition, some students may be performing poorly as a result of environmental, cultural or economic disadvantages, and these factors should be taken into consideration before referring such students for special education consideration. (34 CFR 300.534, 34 CFR 300.543)

Students with Language and Speech Problems

Student with significant problems in language and speech are relatively easy to identify and refer for special education consideration. Some students with *receptive* language disabilities may have difficulty understanding or comprehending language and, as a result, don't respond well to oral directions. Students who are limited in their ability to use oral language to communicate may have an *expressive* language problem. In addition, some students with poorly developed articulation skills are hard to understand. Students with language or speech problems should be referred to the speech therapist to determine if they require speech and language therapy as a special education service. Students who speak a language other than English and are in the process of learning English are not considered students with language problems and should not be referred. (34 CFR 300.7, 34 CFR 300.24)

Students with Learning Problems

Some students who demonstrate significant problems in learning academic material may have cognitive deficits. In the case of students who may have cognitive limitations, you may observe an inability to understand concepts and a tendency to be very literal and concrete. Academic content that is abstract or requires a higher level of thought is often beyond the reasoning abilities of students with limited cognitive abilities. A majority of students with moderate to severe cognitive limitations will be identified as special education students as preschoolers, but there are some students with more mild cognitive impairments who may not be identified until elementary school. In addition, some students with very mild cognitive limitations will continue in general education throughout their school careers. They are students with lower than average intellectual ability, but they are not functioning at levels that render them eligible for special education. These students appear to be age-appropriate in many ways, but may lack the intellectual ability to achieve grade-level academic performance. (34 CFR 300.7, 34 CFR 300.313)

Students who may have learning disabilities that affect their academic achievement often demonstrate an inconsistent pattern of performance, depending upon the skills required to complete an assignment. These students typically have at least average intellectual ability, but demonstrate specific skill deficits in reading, written language or mathematics. There are many ways in which learning disabilities can adversely impact a student's ability to learn academic material. Some students will exhibit problems in visual or auditory memory, while others may be unable to decode and comprehend written material effectively. In some cases, students with learning disabilities develop compensatory skills and adaptive strategies that may, initially, mask their disabilities, but when they encounter increasingly complex and demanding academic tasks, their learning problems may become apparent and limit their achievement. It is not uncommon for some learning disabled students to be a bit defensive in areas where they feel inadequate, and they may be initially resistant to offers of help or support because they do not wish to be singled out for special treatment. It's important to create a safe classroom environment so students with learning problems can feel comfortable to ask for the help they need. (34 CFR 300.7, 34 CFR 300.541)

Students with Emotional Problems

There are students in every classroom who have emotional problems that impact their educational performance. For some students, these problems limit their achievement and prevent them from performing as well as they might. In other cases, a student's emotional problems are so significant that they adversely affect education, and the student may be eligible for special education as emotionally disturbed.

Students who may be emotionally disturbed often function very differently from their peers in the classroom. They may appear preoccupied and somewhat disengaged. In some cases, students will isolate themselves and avoid engagement, while in other situations such students demand attention and act in bizarre ways. You should be aware of students whose emotional responses seem atypical when compared to peers. Whether the student appears aloof, passive and depressed, or manic, overly emotional and grossly inappropriate, the student should be referred for special education assessment. (34 CFR 300.7)

Students with Attention Problems

There are students who should be referred for special education consideration because they have attention problems that adversely affect their education. Some of these students may have a diagnosis of attention deficit disorder (ADD) with or without hyperactivity (ADHD). Students who have been diagnosed with attention deficit disorder and hyperactivity demonstrate an inability to attend and concentrate; they have an extremely mobile attention span and an accompanying high level of physical activity. These students have extreme difficulty sitting still, listening to instruction, and staying on task. They often appear to distract themselves and may be hypersensitive to environmental stimuli. In contrast, students diagnosed with attention deficit disorder without hyperactivity may be calm and placid, but they also are limited in the ability to attend and concentrate. They may appear to be inattentive and disinterested in certain tasks, but engaged in others. They seem to "tune out" at times and can appear passive and distant. Students with a diagnosis of attention deficit disorder with or without hyperactivity should be referred for special education consideration, as well as other students who may not have a diagnosis but appear to match the profile. (34 CFR 300.7)

Students with Physical Problems

Some students have physical problems that qualify them for special education programs and services. Typically, most of these students enter public schools with their special needs already identified. Almost all of the students who are blind, deaf or have orthopedic impairments have been receiving special education services as infants and preschoolers. However, other students with hearing problems, visual impairments and mild orthopedic impairments may enter school unidentified and will need to be referred for assessment when their condition adversely affects their education. In many cases, these physical problems are identified at health screenings that take place prior to kindergarten enrollment, but in some situations, you will need to refer such students for special education assessment. (34 CFR 300.7)

Students with Health Problems

Some students enter school with chronic or acute health problems that may require special education services. Although most students with serious health problems that qualify for special education will have a diagnosis when they enroll, some students may acquire such a problem sometime during their school career. You should be aware that any student who is diagnosed with a serious health problem may need to be referred for special education consideration. Conditions that are named in the IDEA include asthma, attention deficit disorder with and without hyperactivity, diabetes, epilepsy, a heart condition, hemophilia, lead poisoning, leukemia, nephritis, rheumatic fever, and sickle cell anemia. (34 CFR 300.7, 34 CFR 300.24)

Chapter 5

How Are Students Identified for Special Education?

The Short Answer

To be identified for special education, students must be properly evaluated and an Individualized Educational Program team must determine that they meet the eligibility standard for designation as a child with a disability who requires a special education program or service. (34 CFR 300.7)

An Overview of the Identification Process

The identification process begins with a referral for special education consideration from a general educator or parent. Based on the information provided in the referral, if there appears to be evidence that the student may have a suspected disability, the parent is informed in writing that the school district wishes to assess the student. The district sends to the parent a copy of the district's statement of Parent Rights and Procedural Safeguards along with an assessment plan that describes the proposed evaluation process. If the parent signs permission for the assessment, the district will conduct an evaluation within 50 calendar days from the date they received the signed assessment plan and convene an IEP team meeting with the parent to review the results of the evaluation. If the IEP team determines that the student meets the eligibility criteria for one of the disability categories described in the IDEA and requires a special education program or service, the student is identified as a special education student. (34 CFR 300.125, 34 CFR 300.320, 34 CFR 300.343, 34 CFR 300.530-543)

IDEA Disability Categories

Under IDEA, students are identified as eligible for special education based upon a designated category of disability that adversely affects educational performance. The categories of disability are intended to merely describe the primary nature of the student's disability. Since special education program funding levels are linked to the severity of the students' disabilities, it is necessary to be able to describe, categorize and count the students with different disabling conditions. (34 CFR 300.7)

Autism

Usually evident before age 3, autism is a developmental disability that affects verbal and nonverbal communication and social interaction. Students with autism may be very interested in repetitive activities, resist change in routines, and may respond in unusual ways to physical or sensory experiences. In comparison to their peers, they may appear disinterested in social interaction and may not initiate communication. Group activities may be problematic for such students, and they often seek to isolate themselves. Some students with autism actively resist shifting tasks and have preferred activities. Most will require help and structure during transitions from one thing to the next.

Hearing-Impaired or Deaf

A student with a hearing impairment has a permanent or fluctuating hearing loss that adversely affects educational performance, but is not as severe as deafness. A student who is considered to be deaf has a hearing loss so severe that processing language through hearing, with or without amplification, adversely affects his or her educational performance. A majority of students with hearing impairment or deafness are identified with these disabilities before age 3, as their rate of language development is delayed when compared with their peers.

Emotionally Disturbed

Students with an emotional disturbance display behaviors and characteristics that are quite different from their peers and adversely affect their educational performance. To be eligible under this category, the district must observe one or more of the following characteristics over a long period of time and to a marked degree:

- An inability to learn that cannot be explained by intellectual, sensory or health factors.

- An inability to build or maintain satisfactory interpersonal relationships with peers and teachers.

- Inappropriate types of behaviors or feelings under normal circumstances.

- A general pervasive mood of unhappiness or depression.

- A tendency to develop physical symptoms or fears associated with personal or school problems.

Students diagnosed with schizophrenia are included as emotionally disturbed. Students, who are diagnosed as socially maladjusted, without evidence of one or more of the characteristics listed above, are not considered to be emotionally disturbed.

Students who are emotionally disturbed often behave in ways that are atypical when compared to their peers. They may appear to be preoccupied and distant or display emotional outbursts that are uncontrolled and unpredictable. Often they are difficult to direct and may demonstrate aggressive and inappropriate behaviors with little regard for consequences. They are often impulsive and may not recognize situations that are dangerous. Some students may have difficulty distinguishing between fantasy and reality, while others may experience significant mood swings within a short period of time.

Other Health Impaired

Some students may have a chronic or acute health problem such as asthma, attention deficit disorder or attention deficit hyperactivity disorder, diabetes, epilepsy, a heart condition, hemophilia, lead poisoning, leukemia, nephritis, rheumatic fever, or sickle cell anemia that adversely affects educational performance as a result of limited strength, vitality or alertness, including a heightened alertness to environmental stimuli in the educational setting.

Many of these students are diagnosed with a medical condition that is known prior to their enrollment in public school, but some students' medical conditions will be identified during their school career. It is possible for a student to be diagnosed with one of the conditions identified, but it does not have an adverse impact on the student's education. In such cases, the student may not be found eligible for special education.

Orthopedic Impairment

Students who have a severe orthopedic impairment caused by congenital anomaly or disease or from other causes may be eligible for special education if there is an adverse impact upon their educational performance.

Most typically, such students may have limitations in mobility, fine and gross motor functioning, communication and self-care as a result of their orthopedic impairment. These students may or may not have limitations in cognitive ability. Some students will participate in general education classes with minimal special education support, while others may require a specialized educational program.

Mental Retardation or Developmental Delay

Students ages 3 to 9 may be identified as developmentally delayed if they demonstrate delays in physical development, cognitive development, communication development, social or emotional development, or adaptive development when compared with their peers. Students who demonstrate significantly sub-average general intellectual functioning, existing concurrently with deficits in adaptive behavior and manifested during the developmental period may be identified as mentally retarded.

Students with developmental delay and mental retardation will demonstrate significant lags in age-appropriate skills when compared with their peers and will require special education support throughout their public school careers. Some of these students will be identified as disabled at birth, and most will be identified before age 3.

Specific Learning Disability

Students who are identified with a specific learning disability have a disorder in one or more of the psychological processes involved in understanding or using spoken or written language and that may manifest itself in an imperfect ability to listen, think, speak, read, write, spell or do mathematical calculations. This category can include conditions such as perceptual disabilities, brain injury, minimal brain dysfunction, dyslexia and developmental aphasia. Students not considered to have a specific learning disability are those with learning problems resulting from visual, hearing or motor disabilities;

mental retardation; emotional disturbance; or environmental, cultural or economic disadvantages.

These students may not appear to be different from their peers at birth or at the start of their school careers, but as their learning disability adversely affects their educational performance in specific academic areas, they are identified and enter special education.

Speech and Language Impaired

Students who have communication disorders, such as stuttering, impaired articulation, language impairment or a voice impairment that adversely affects their educational performance are considered to be speech and language impaired.

Depending upon the severity of their speech and language problems, students may be identified prior to age 3. For many students, speech and language problems are not evident until the student enters public school. Because there is a normal variation in students' language development, mild speech and language problems may not be identified until kindergarten or first-grade.

Traumatic Brain Injury

Students who have an acquired injury to the brain caused by an external physical force that results in total or partial functional disability, or psychosocial impairment, or both are eligible for special education based on a traumatic brain injury. The term applies to open and closed head injuries resulting in impairments in one or more areas, such as cognition, language, memory, attention, reasoning, abstract thinking, judgment, problem-solving, psychosocial behavior, physical functions, information processing, speech, and sensory, perceptual and motor abilities. Traumatic brain injury does not apply to brain injuries that are congenital or degenerative, or to brain injuries induced by birth trauma.

These students are almost always victims of accidents that result in traumatic brain injury, and their need for special education programs and/or services will vary, both in terms of how much support they may need as well as how long they will require services.

In the majority of cases, these students were not identified as requiring special education programs and/or services prior to the accident that resulted in traumatic brain injury.

Visual Impairment Including Blindness

Students with a visual impairment that, even with correction, adversely affects educational performance are eligible for special education. Students may have partial sight or blindness.

In most cases, the student's degree of visual impairment will determine when he or she is identified as needing special education. Students who are blind at birth will be immediately identified and referred for infant services, while other students whose visual impairments become evident as toddlers or preschoolers will receive services at that point. Some students with more subtle visual impairments will be identified when their disability interferes with their academic progress.

Chapter 6

What Happens in an IEP Meeting?

The Short Answer

As envisioned under the IDEA, an individualized education program (IEP) meeting is the legally mandated decision-making process
for determining eligibility and the educational programming and services for students with disabilities. The required members of an IEP
team include the parent, an administrator, a special education teacher,
the general education teacher of the student, and, if appropriate, the
student. The IEP team determines special education eligibility, develops the content of the IEP, reviews annual progress, decides if an exit
from special education is appropriate, and participates in disciplinary
proceedings such as lengthy suspensions or proposed expulsions
involving special education students. (34 CFR 300.340-350, 34 CFR
300.523)

The Structure of an IEP Meeting

The IEP meeting is designed to address all of the specific legal
requirements under IDEA and, as a result, has a predictable structure.
In some school districts, written agendas are distributed at the beginning of the meeting outlining the topics to be covered so that the IEP
team stays on task. In other districts, the sequence of the meeting is
simply described by the chairperson of the IEP meeting. Initial IEP
meetings generally follow the same steps:

- Introduce the IEP team.
- Distribute to the parent a copy of Parent Rights and Proce-
  dural Safeguards.
- Review assessment results and establish present levels of
  performance.
- Determine eligibility for special education.
- Draft goals and benchmarks.

- Identify the specific program that is appropriate to implement the goals.

- Describe any related services.

- Note any supplementary aids or services, including considering the need for assistive technology.

- Describe participation in the general education curriculum.

- Determine participation in state assessment programs.

- Determine the need for extended school year.

- Transition planning, if appropriate.

- Sign the IEP and distribute copies to all participants.

Although the sequence is simple, each phase has a specific legal purpose and rationale.

For IEP meetings that are not initial IEP meetings, the sequence may be adjusted to reflect the specific purpose of the meeting. Purposes can include an annual review, a proposed change of program or service, modifications of goals or objectives, a review of proposed disciplinary action, an exit from special education or any other purpose that requires an IEP meeting. (34 CFR 300.340-350, 34 CFR 300.523)

Why You Are a Required Member of the IEP Team

When Congress reauthorized the IDEA in 1997, general education teachers were specifically named as required members of all IEP teams for special education students enrolled in their classes or who might be enrolled in their classes. The rationale for this change is to make sure general education teachers participate in the development of the IEP, are knowledgeable about the contents of the IEP, and are able to provide input to the IEP team regarding any supplementary aids or services the student needs to be able to participate in the general curriculum. Because the majority of special education students participated in general education classes and the general curriculum to some degree, the law expanded the role of general educators, reflecting their increased responsibilities to educate students with disabilities.

As a mandatory member of the IEP team, you are expected to contribute your observations of the special education student's performance in your class so that the IEP accurately reflects the student's engagement and participation in the general curriculum. In addition, by participating in the development of the IEP, you are expected to implement any goals that involve your classroom setting, such as behavior plans or accommodations and modifications of the general curriculum. As a member of the IEP team reviewing any proposed disciplinary action involving a special education student in your class, you bring informed observations of the student's day-to-day behavior that may be helpful in determining if there is a relationship between the student's disability and the behavior in question. (34 CFR 300.340-350, 34 CFR 300.523)

Preparing for the IEP Meeting

As the general education teacher on the IEP team, you'll need to do some preparation to participate effectively. In many IEP team meetings, you will be asked to comment on the student's performance, so it would be helpful for you to give some thought to how you would describe the student's participation in your class. It's useful to focus upon concrete details that illustrate how the student approaches assigned tasks and handles the interpersonal demands of the classroom setting. You should be prepared to offer some examples of any behavioral issues that might be interfering with learning or comment on peer relationships, if that is an issue. It's not necessary to develop a written report, but it is a good idea to jot down some notes so that you can make sure to cover the issues you feel are important. If there are questions regarding the student's academic progress, you might bring some samples of the student's work, along with work samples typical of students in your class, masking out names, so that the team can draw realistic comparisons. If the student's IEP requires you to gather data or maintain logs or notes, you should bring those to the IEP meeting and be prepared to speak about them. If a behavior plan is part of the student's IEP, you should describe your efforts to implement the plan. In some situations, you may be asked to complete a rating sheet or checklist in advance of the IEP meeting, and it would be a good idea for you to keep a copy and bring it to the meeting. It's important for you to remember that you are a trained professional who has subject area expertise as well as an understanding of student behaviors that result in success in your classroom. As a general educator, your input is invaluable to the IEP team and can contribute to developing an IEP that supports the special education student's efforts to achieve goals.

Chapter 7

Why You Need to Know What Is Written on the IEP

The Short Answer

The Individuals with Disabilities Education Act, or IDEA, is a federal law. Failure to implement the special education student's IEP is illegal. When you are assigned specific responsibilities in an IEP, refusing or neglecting to do them can expose you and your district to legal action.

As a general educator, you are required by law to be knowledgeable regarding the contents of the IEP of each special education student enrolled in your classes, and you are legally obligated to implement any portions of an IEP that apply to you. (34 CFR 300.343-347)

Elementary & Secondary Schools Are Different

Although the legal requirements of IDEA do not differentiate between elementary schools and secondary schools, general educators working in these different settings face unique challenges in meeting their legal responsibilities to special education students.

At the elementary-school level, you are assigned to a specified grade level and provide all of the academic instruction to a class of typically less than 32 pupils, including two or three special education students. As an elementary educator, you work with your students for up to six hours every weekday, and, over the course of a year, create a close bond with each of them. Your relationship with the students in your class is intense, and you are knowledgeable about every aspect of their school life. In many cases, you also have a relationship with most of the parents of your students and may conference with them once or twice year. Your high level of involvement with your students enables you to help the IEP team develop realistic goals and appropriate activities to be implemented in your classroom. At the elementary level, you are challenged to respond to the many competing demands for your time and attention. Your success will depend upon your ability to develop strategies that enable you to meet your legal responsibilities to the special education students while you also address the instructional needs of the rest of your class.

At the secondary level, you are one of many educators within an academic department, teaching specific courses to groups of students assigned by grade level. Typically, you will teach five or six 50- to 60-minute classes of up to 35 students per class, including special education students, and work with as many as 150 to 165 students per day. You may have the same students all year or you may change classes once or twice during the year, depending upon how the school year is organized. Your involvement with students varies, but the sheer volume of students you teach limits the intensity of your interaction. You know how the student is performing in your class, but you may not know very much about how the student is functioning in other areas. Your contact with most students' parents is infrequent and limited. In some cases, you will be selected as the general educator assigned to one of your student's IEP teams, and you will assist in the development of that student's IEP. Your knowledge of the student is limited to your observations of the student's performance in your class, and your role is that of a general education representative. In some cases, you will not participate on the IEP team of a special education student assigned to your class; some other general educator will serve as the general education representative on the IEP team. The challenges you face as a general educator at the secondary level are related to the numbers of students you teach and the potential communication and logistical problems associated with large, departmentalized secondary schools. It is no surprise that the majority of allegations of noncompliance and failure to appropriately implement IEPs involve secondary schools, and they are directly related to district size and complexity. To successfully meet your responsibilities under the IDEA, you must read the IEP for each of the special education students in your classes, understand the students' education condition and their instructional needs, and know what specific activities have been assigned to you and your classroom. (34 CFR 300.343-347)

The IEP Is Not a Guarantee

IEPs developed for special education students are documents that describe the programs and services the school district agrees to provide. The IEP is a formal, written statement of the intent of the parties. When a team writes an IEP that describes instructional goals and activities to be conducted by general educators, there is an assumption that because you were part of the IEP team, you will make a good faith effort to address those goals and implement those activities. There is no guarantee the goals will be met or the activities will be successful, but there is a reasonable expectation of cooperation and compliance on your part. When parents make allegations of noncompliance and failure to implement the IEP, hearing officers and courts look for evidence that the school district staff attempted to comply with the content of the IEP. You must understand that you are expected to keep the agreements documented on the IEP, but that you will not be held liable if the child does not attain the stated goals.

Chapter 8

How to Handle Accommodations, Modifications and Standards

The Short Answer

Districts provide students with IEP-prescribed accommodations and/or modifications to enable them to be involved in and progress in the general curriculum, and to participate in state or district-wide assessments. Accommodations do not fundamentally alter or lower the standards for the course or test, and students using accommodations receive credit toward a standard diploma. In contrast, modifications do fundamentally alter or lower the standard for a course or test, and the student may not receive credit toward a standard diploma. (34 CFR 300.347; *Letter to Anonymous,* 22 IDELR 456 (OSEP 1995))

Accommodations

IDEA requires you to provide to special education students in your class the accommodations listed on students' IEPs. The purpose of the accommodation is to enable the student to access the general curriculum and demonstrate his knowledge of course-content by making an adjustment to the way the student shows his or her understanding. The accommodation enables special education students to demonstrate mastery of the content while minimizing the impact of their disability. Ideally, the accommodation described on the IEP permits the student to compete in the class on an equal footing with non-disabled students by providing an alteration in the means of demonstrating academic skill. As a result, the accommodation does not fundamentally alter or lower the standards of the course or test.

For a student with fine motor problems that interfere with handwriting, an example of a typical accommodation might be to provide additional time to write responses on an essay test. By granting more time, limitations posed by the student's rate of production are minimized, and his or her ability to demonstrate understanding of content is enhanced. Another common accommodation allows a student with a visual impairment to take a test with fewer mathematics problems on each page. By reducing the amount of visual stimuli on each page, the student can focus on the problems without experiencing visual overload. The student's math test will have more pages, but the pages are easier for the student to read.

These examples of accommodations reflect adjustments to how students demonstrate their understanding, because they increase the likelihood that the students' performances accurately reflect their knowledge of the academic material. Accommodations reduce the impact of the disabilities while increasing the validity of academic assessments.

Modifications

Some special education students require modifications of course-content, assignments and tests that lower the standards for the course, but enable them to access some portions of the general curriculum and participate in the class. Typically, students who require IEP-based modifications of course-content, assignments or assessments to participate in regular classes have disabilities that limit their ability to progress at the same rate as other students in the class. When special education students with significant limitations in their academic abilities enroll in general education classes with modifications, the IEP team recognizes that the student will not obtain credit toward a standard diploma, and there is no expectation that the student is meeting the district or state standards for the class. In many cases, the IEP document will note that modifications of district or state assessments or coursework will not meet diploma requirements, and the parents agree to this provision when they sign the IEP.

Examples of modifications include a simplified curriculum; shortened assignments and assigned work at lower levels of difficulty; modified grading standards; partial credit; simpler and shorter assessments; and elimination of standards-based course requirements such as mandatory reading lists, lab requirements, etc. Since the purpose of IEP-based modifications is to enable students with disabilities to participate in general education classes and access portions of the general curriculum, you are not responsible for providing these students with the same standards-based course you offer to nondisabled students.

Standards & Diplomas

States and school districts establish the standards that students must meet to graduate with a standard diploma; they are not required to alter or lower the standards for students with disabilities. You are expected to provide standards-based instruction to students enrolled in your classes and to award passing grades only to those students who meet the standards for the course. At the same time, special education students may enroll in your class(es), bringing with them IEP-based modifications that lower the standards for the course. How can these differences be reconciled?

To begin with, let's assume you teach high school courses, based upon state and district standards, to students who are diploma-bound. Special education students who enroll in your standards-based classes with IEP-based modifications that lower the standards for the course will not obtain credit toward a diploma. As a result, you can implement IEP-based modifications and provide the student an opportunity to participate in the general curriculum, but with altered content that does not meet the standards for the course. Parents of students with disabilities must be informed, in advance, that IEP-based modifications that fundamentally alter or lower the standards for a class will not meet state and district standards for a diploma, so that they can understand the consequences of the IEP team decisions.

Chapter 9

Can I Give Special Education Students Failing Grades?

The Short Answer

You can give special education students failing grades, but you must be sure the reason the student is failing the class is *not* because you failed to provide the IDEA-mandated "free, appropriate public education" or FAPE. You must provide special education students enrolled in your class any IEP-approved accommodations and/or modifications that are appropriate to the general education class, as well as the program, services and supports described in the IEP. If, in spite of providing the IEP program and services, the student does not take advantage of the opportunity to learn, and you can document that the student has not met your grading criteria to pass the class because of the student's lack of cooperation, participation or preparation, you can fail the student. (34 CFR 300.300, 34 CFR 300.347)

The Disability Cannot Cause the Failing Grade

Students whom the district has determined to be disabled under IDEA require special education programs and services to meet their educational needs. Because these students have been designated as disabled, it is illegal to discriminate against them as a result of their disabilities, and you, as their teacher, cannot fail them because they are disabled. It is important for you to demonstrate, if challenged, that the failing grade is not caused by their disability, but by some factors that are unrelated to their disabling condition.

In addition, you should not fail the special education student if you have not implemented all of the accommodations and modifications recommended by the IEP team as appropriate to your class. In some cases, the student's disability may not have an adverse impact upon the skills needed to pass your class. For example, a student who has a learning disability that affects written language may not require accommodations or modifications for a math class. As the math teacher, you may find that the student has demonstrated the ability to learn the content and complete the assignments, but the student is not motivated to do the work or refuses to do the work and, as a result, earns a failing grade.

If the IEP team has determined that the special education student has behaviors that impede learning or the learning of others, the IEP will include positive behavioral interventions and supports to address that behavior. You should make sure that you have implemented any behavior interventions that are included in the IEP; you cannot fail the student because of these behaviors. In such cases, it is more appropriate to request an IEP meeting to address the issue and formulate a strategy.

Providing the Opportunity to Learn

Special education students are not guaranteed passing grades, but they must be provided the opportunity to learn and obtain some educational benefit from their classes. As a result, you must demonstrate that you have provided the student with an opportunity to learn in your class and that you have made a good-faith effort to enable the student to obtain some educational benefit from your instruction. For a failing student, you must be able to document that despite your efforts to create a classroom environment that is conducive to learning, the student has chosen not to cooperate and did not take advantage of the educational opportunities you provided. You should be prepared to compile the written evidence of the student's lack of effort and participation so that, if challenged, you can demonstrate why the student has failed the class.

A Role for the IEP Team

Typically, the IEP team is responsible for monitoring the special education student's progress on an annual basis. But when the student is in danger of failing classes, an IEP team meeting is probably needed. The purpose of the IEP team meeting would be to enable the general education teacher to present the problem and seek assistance from the IEP team in determining what needs to be done. By requesting an IEP team meeting to discuss the student's lack of cooperation or participation, or to adjust some aspect of the IEP, you are being proactive and attempting to address the problem. Inviting the student to the IEP team meeting is helpful because the student needs to be held accountable for the lack of cooperation and encouraged to improve class participation so he or she can benefit from the educational program. In many cases, requesting the involvement of the IEP team, with the student in attendance, is a powerful strategy to demonstrate to the student the support that is available to help him or her succeed.

Chapter 10

How Are Special Education Students Disciplined?

The Short Answer

Special education students may be disciplined like any other student for up to 10 days a year. When a special education student is removed from school for more than 10 days, there are a series of special protections and procedures that must be followed to ensure that the behavior that results in discipline is not caused by the student's disability.

Students with Disabilities Are Treated Differently

Like nondisabled students, students with special needs sometimes are involved in behavior that may require you to recommend disciplinary action, such as suspension from school. In the case of minor misbehaviors, there may be little difference between the disciplinary consequences for special education students and their general education peers. Because the special education student has been identified as a "child with a disability," in some situations you will need to treat them differently. (34 CFR 300.7, 34 CFR 300.520)

Short-term Suspensions of 10 Days or Less

School authorities can suspend a special education student for up to 10 days or less for violations of school rules, without parental consent. During this period of time, the school district is not required to provide any services, so long as it would not provide services to a nondisabled student who are similarly suspended. (34 CFR 300.520)

Short-term Suspensions of 10 Days or More, Not a Change of Placement

Special education students suspended beyond 10 days receive services and additional protections and procedures not available to their general education peers. When a student with a disability is suspended more than 10 days, beginning on the 11th day the school district must provide educational services that will enable the student to progress in the general curriculum and to advance toward meeting the IEP goals. The school administration will consult with the student's special education teacher to determine the extent to which services are needed to help the student progress. In addition, the school principal reviews the suspension and determines whether or not the suspension constitutes a pattern of exclusion that represents a "change of placement." To make this determination, the principal reviews the length of each removal, the total number of removal days, and the proximity of the removals to each other. Within 10 days after the 11th total day of disciplinary removals in a school year, an IEP team meeting must be held to plan for a "functional behavior assessment," an evaluation that analyzes and describes the function of the student's problem behavior. The team then develops a "behavior intervention plan," a written plan that is part of the IEP and attempts to intervene, modify and redirect problem behavior. If these elements already are in the student's IEP, the team reviews them and revises them, as needed, to address the problem behavior. The IEP team reviews the IEP and determines the educational services the student will receive while assigned to the disciplinary setting. (34 CFR 300.121, 34 CFR 300.520)

Suspensions of 10 Days or More, Considered a Change of Placement

There are circumstances when a special education student will receive suspensions that exceed 10 days and that *are* considered a "change of placement." In these situations, typically reserved for serious behavioral problems that may include weapons and drugs, the procedural requirements are more stringent, and the protections offered to the disabled student are more comprehensive.

The parents are provided with a notice of the proposed disciplinary action and a copy of Parent Rights and Procedural Safeguards. An IEP team meeting is convened within 10 days after the initial removal day, and the IEP team must conduct a "manifestation determination." The purpose of the manifestation determination is to carefully make several judgments regarding the behavior in question. The team must decide if 1) the behavior for which the special education student is being disciplined was caused by the student's disability, 2) the IEP and program was appropriate at the time of the behavior, 3) all necessary services and supports named in the IEP were provided, and 4) the student's disability impaired his or her ability to understand the impact and consequences of the behavior or the ability to control the behavior. If the IEP team finds that the problem behavior was a manifestation of the student's disability, the proposed disciplinary action cannot take place. If, however, the IEP finds, as a result of the manifestation determination, that the behavior was not a manifestation of the student's disability, the student is subject to discipline in the same manner as a general education student who engaged in the same behavior. In addition, if the IEP team finds that the school district did not conduct a functional behavior assessment, as described above, before the behavior that resulted in the removal, the IEP team must develop an assessment plan for the functional behavior assessment and the development of a behavior intervention plan, also described above. If, however, there was a functional behavior assessment and a behavior intervention plan, the IEP team revises them to address the behavior. The IEP team also must determine the educational services the student will receive while assigned to the disciplinary setting. (34 CFR 300.121, 34 CFR 300.519-529)

Removals for Weapons & Drugs

Students with disabilities who violate weapon and drug policies may be removed from their current placements and assigned to an interim alternative educational setting for up to 45 days without parental consent. When students are found to be in possession of weapons or drugs on the school campus, school authorities may report these acts as crimes and notify local law enforcement agencies. (34 CFR 300.121, 34 CFR 300.520, 34 CFR 300.529)

Removals to Prevent Injury

If school authorities have substantial evidence that a special education student should be removed from the current placement because keeping the student in that placement is substantially likely to result in injury to the student or to others, the school district must ask an administrative hearing officer to order the student to an interim, alternative educational setting for up to 45 days. In making such a decision, the hearing officer must consider the appropriateness of the current placement, whether the public agency has made reasonable efforts to minimize the risk of harm, including providing supplementary aids and services, and whether the proposed placement meets the legal criteria for an interim alternative educational setting. (34 CFR 300.521)

Interim Alternative Educational Setting

Students with disabilities can be assigned to an interim alternative educational setting (IAES) for up to 45 days for weapon or drug violations, or when an administrative hearing officer rules that substantial evidence reveals that an injury to the student or others is substantially likely to take place if the student remains in the current placement. When a student is assigned to the IAES, the IEP team decides where the setting will be and how the student will continue to progress in the general curriculum, receive services needed to meet IEP goals, and any services needed to prevent the behavior from recurring. (34 CFR 300.121, 34 CFR 300.520-522)

Expulsion

Special education students may be expelled from school only when 1) an IEP team has determined that the behavior was not a manifestation of the student's disability and 2) the student had a functional behavior assessment and a behavior intervention plan that was appropriate. Once the IEP team determines that the behavior was not a manifestation of the student's disability, the special education student may be expelled if a nondisabled student would be expelled in a similar circumstance. In the case of a special education student, educational services must be provided to the extent the student's IEP team determines necessary to enable the student to progress in the general curriculum and advance toward the IEP goals. (34 CFR 300.121, 34 CFR 300.520)

Parent Appeal Rights

With the exception of suspensions of less than 10 days and weapon and drug violations, parents retain their same special education appeal rights during disciplinary actions that involve special education students. The IEP team meetings that are required for discipline purposes provide the very same parent rights and procedural safeguards as any other special education context. (34 CFR 300.525-529)

Chapter 11

What Notes and Documentation Do I Need to Maintain?

The Short Answer

Disputes regarding whether a special education student has received a "free, appropriate public education," known as FAPE, may be resolved in administrative hearings or court proceedings that rely upon written evidence to determine whether the school district followed correct procedures and provided the program and services the student required. As a general educator working with students with disabilities, you need to maintain notes and records that can document your efforts to implement the student's individualized education program, or IEP. (34 CFR 300.509, 34 CFR 300.512)

Start with Your Current System

You probably have some system of notes and documentation to assist you to plan instruction, assign work, report attendance, record grades, and respond to written and telephone inquiries from parents, colleagues and administrators. The current system you have in place, augmented by specific elements required under the IEP and an activity log, will form the basis of your documentation efforts.

Examine the IEP

You are required to be knowledgeable regarding the contents of IEPs for each special education student assigned to your class. You should have a copy of that IEP for your reference and to help you develop your system of notes and documentation. When you review the IEP, you should make a list of any goals, accommodations and modifications, behavior intervention plans, and supplementary aids or services that apply to your classroom setting. You'll want to be able to document, in writing, your implementation of all portions of the student's IEP that involve your class. In many cases, your current system

47

may be adequate to address references to attendance, assignments and grading, but you may need to make additions or modifications to your system to address specific elements of the IEP that your current system does not accommodate. For example, if the student's IEP includes accommodations or modifications of assignments or tests, it's a good idea for you to keep a copy of those assignments or tests that show the accommodations or modifications you've made to the original assignments. If the student's IEP includes a behavior plan to be implemented in your classroom, you should have a copy of the plan and maintain a running record of your interventions based upon the plan. In addition to activities required by the student's IEP, you also should keep track of any consultations or conferences you have with staff and administration regarding the student and her participation in your class. Discussions with the student's counselor, special education teacher, speech therapist or school psychologist should be noted and maintained for your records. (34 CFR 300.342, 34 CFR 300.346-347)

Activity Logs

It is often helpful to create an activity log for each student with a disability in your class. The log serves to document phone calls, conferences and any action you take on behalf of the student. The format of the log is simple and straightforward, with columns for the date, time, and description of the activity. A loose-leaf binder that contains a page for each student is one method that's easy to use. When a call comes in or you contact the parent, you make a note on the activity log to document what you've done. If there is ever a question regarding what did or didn't happen, you've got a written record that documents your action.

Work Samples

Whenever there is a question regarding progress or achievement, a work sample provides effective documentation that often resolves the question. You may already maintain samples of student work as part of your system of assessment. If so, you have documentation of the special education student's performance. If, however, you don't keep samples of student work, you should begin to maintain periodic work samples for each of your special education students. It is useful to collect these samples on a quarterly basis to reveal any changes in the student's achievement over time. It is particularly important to maintain work samples that reflect the implementation of any IEP-mandated accommodations or modifications.

Notes, Letters and Reports

It's a good idea to keep copies of notes and letters (and your responses) you receive from parents, colleagues, administrators, outside professionals and agencies regarding special education students. You should even keep informal notes so that they are available, if needed, should there be a question regarding a communication involving the student. It is particularly important for you to date any written communication you receive and your response, so that you can demonstrate a prompt reply.

If you are asked to complete a rating sheet or narrative report on behalf of a special education student, you should ask for written confirmation that the parent has granted permission for you to provide the information requested. When you receive a copy of the parent's permission, you should date it and keep it in your file along with the original request and a copy of any information that you provided.

In general, when responding to requests for information, your reply should be within the scope of your training and experience as a general educator. Avoid using any terms that you do not have the professional qualifications to defend. You should be aware that anything you write regarding a special education student will, if there is a dispute, become part of the body of evidence in a hearing or legal proceeding.

Chapter 12

When Should I Call an IEP Meeting?

The Short Answer

Under the IDEA, each school district is responsible for initiating and conducting meetings for the purpose of developing, reviewing and revising the IEP of a student with a disability. As a general educator who has a special education student enrolled in your class, you should request an IEP meeting whenever you believe a review of the content or implementation of the IEP is appropriate. (34 CFR 300.343-350)

Concerns Regarding the Content of the IEP

Concerns that you have regarding the content of the IEP may include goal statements, accommodations or modifications, behavior intervention plans, supplementary aids and services, or other elements of the IEP that you may be required to follow. It's important to note that the IEP is a proposed program that can, and should, be modified if there are questions regarding either the meaning or accuracy of the document. As the general education teacher on the IEP team, it's important to make sure that what's written in the IEP is understandable and realistic. Although the IEP does not guarantee the goals will be achieved, it should clearly describe a program that is likely to result in some educational benefit for the student. If you have questions regarding your responsibilities as drafted in the IEP, it is better to raise those concerns as soon as possible so they can be discussed and the document can be modified if appropriate.

Concerns Regarding Implementation of the IEP

In some cases, you will have concerns regarding whether the IEP is being properly implemented. If, for example, the student is truant from school, the IEP is not being implemented, and an IEP meeting should be held to develop an appropriate intervention to improve attendance. In another case, if the student refuses to do homework and participate in required classroom activities, it would be appropriate to request an IEP meeting to discuss these problems and develop some strategies to improve cooperation and compliance. It is important to document your concerns if there are barriers to IEP implementation, because participation in general education classes and access to the general curriculum are considered part of many special education students' legal entitlement to a "free, appropriate public education." If the student's parents allege a denial of FAPE, your IEP notes would document that you and the school district made a good-faith effort to implement the IEP.

If you have concerns that a special education student's placement in your class is inappropriate, it is an issue of IEP implementation. For example, if a special education student's behavior is erratic and unpredictable, creating classroom disturbances that interfere with your ability to teach, you should request an IEP meeting to determine if placement in your class is viable. By requesting an IEP meeting when a special education student's behavior is problematic, you let the IEP team know that the present program is not working. Based upon your information, the IEP team can review the program and decide if further assessment is indicated, additional services are needed, or whether the placement is inappropriate and should be discontinued.

As a general educator, your candid assessment of the special education student's ability to meet the academic and behavioral expectations of your classroom is vital to the IEP team's ability to realistically evaluate student progress. Without your feedback, the IEP team cannot gauge the effectiveness of the student's program and cannot provide you with the support you need to implement the IEP.

Chapter 13

How Are Disputes Resolved in Special Education?

The Short Answer

It is inevitable that parents and school districts will have differences of opinion regarding aspects of special education procedures and programs. From debates over initial identification and eligibility to concerns regarding whether the program offered is appropriate, special education decisions can be controversial. As a general educator with students with disabilities enrolled in your classes, you may be required to participate in legal proceedings to resolve disputes involving special education procedures, programs or services. (34 CFR 300.506-514)

IDEA Provides Several Venues to Resolve Disagreements

The IDEA recognizes that there may be legitimate differences of opinion between parents and school district staff regarding the entire special education process — from referral to the development and implementation of individualized education programs, or IEPs. As a result, there is a comprehensive system available to resolve disagreements. It includes mediation, administrative due process hearings, and appeals to federal court. All of the procedures for resolving disagreements are described in the Parent Rights and Procedural Safeguards document that is initially sent to parents at the point of referral and distributed at every IEP meeting. In addition to formal procedures of mediation and due process hearings, some school districts have established less-formal methods, sometimes referred to as "alternative dispute resolution" procedures. The alternative dispute resolution procedures provide methods to resolve disagreements without resorting to the formal IDEA procedures. The use of alternative dispute resolution methods is voluntary and does not prevent the parties from seeking mediation and/or a due process hearing. (34 CFR 300.503-514)

Mediation

In special education dispute resolution, mediation refers to a specialized problem-solving method that involves a neutral third party who attempts to resolve the disagreements between the parent and the school district. Typically, a mediator is assigned to a case when a parent or school district files for an administrative hearing, but there are some jurisdictions where mediation may be requested without filing for a due process hearing at the state level. Regardless of how the mediator becomes involved, the process is almost always the same. The parties will meet and describe the student, the situation and the nature of the disagreement. The mediator will listen to all of the parties and may, at some point, separate the parties to obtain additional information. When the mediator meets with the parties separately, it is called a caucus. During a caucus, the mediator may ask questions, obtain additional information, or share information she has received from the other parties. It is common for the mediator to ask if she may share information received during a caucus, to ensure that she does not reveal anything that either party wishes to keep confidential. Conversations in mediation and the mediation agreement cannot be part of a due process hearing, so the parties can speak freely without worrying that they will say something that could be used against them if they turn to a due process hearing. The mediator does not and cannot rule in favor of one of the parties, relying instead on the cooperation of the parties to obtain an agreement that will resolve the problem. Sometimes the mediator is successful in resolving the issues and the parties solve their problems. Mediation is an opportunity for both parties to settle their differences and keep the decision-making process in their hands; once they move on to a due process hearing, the final resolution is up to the hearing officer.

If you are involved in mediation as a general educator, your role will be to provide information to the mediator regarding the student's participation and performance in your classroom. If you are asked to participate in mediation on behalf of your school district, the district administrator responsible for supervising special education programs will provide you with information and support. (34 CFR 300.506)

Due Process Hearings

The administrative process for resolving a dispute in special education is called a due process hearing. Once a parent or school district has requested a due process hearing, called a filing, the student's placement does not change, even if the dispute is over placement. This is referred to as "stay-put"; the student continues in the current placement under the IEP until the outcome of the hearing process. Once the hearing officer renders a decision, the student's placement may continue or may be changed as a result of the decision. Once the state receives the filing, a hearing officer is appointed who will conduct the formal hearing that will result in a decision that is binding upon the parties. The due process hearing is like a less-formal court procedure. The parties do not have to be represented by attorneys, but in many cases they have legal counsel. Each party submits the issues they wish resolved and a statement of the resolution they are seeking. In addition, each party must furnish the other party with a list of witnesses they may call and a copy of the evidence that they will submit. During the hearing, each party may choose to make an opening statement, present written evidence, call witnesses, question each other's witnesses, and make a closing statement. The legal rules of evidence may not always apply, and the hearing officer works cooperatively with the parties to make sure that all the relevant facts are heard.

If you are asked to participate in a due process hearing, you will be asked to testify regarding your knowledge, interaction and observations of the student who is the subject of the hearing. It is likely that you will meet with your district's special education director and legal counsel so they can review your testimony and prepare you to be a witness in the hearing. When you are called as a witness, the district's attorney will ask you a series of questions regarding your work with the student. This is called direct testimony. After the questioning by the district's attorney, you may be cross-examined by the parents' attorney. Following the cross-examination, the district's attorney may ask you other questions, called re-direct testimony. In some situations, the hearing officer may ask you questions, either during your direct testimony, cross-examination or on re-direct. Typically the hearings are closed to the public, so confidentiality is not an issue. After the hearing officer has heard the testimony and reviewed the evidence, he will, within a few weeks or months, write a decision that resolves the issue. The hearing officer's decision determines which party prevailed on the issues to be decided. The questions of prevailing party status are important because attorney's fees are available to the parents if they prevail in the hearing. The hearing officer's decision is intended to settle the issue between the parties. If either party is unhappy with the decision, they may appeal to federal court to overturn the hearing officer's decision. (34 CFR 300.507-514)

Appeals to Federal Court

If a parent or school district is unhappy with the hearing officer's decision, they may decide to file an appeal in federal court in the hope of reversing the hearing decision. In most cases, the due process hearing will resolve the matter, but sometimes one of the parties will exercise the right to an appeal. The decision to file an appeal to federal court is significant and can be costly to both parents and school districts. Just as in the due process hearing, parents can recover attorney's fees if they are successful on appeal. If the parents do not prevail, they receive no reimbursement for attorney's fees.

Unlike the due process hearing, a federal appeal process is a very formal process heard in a federal district court in the school district's state. A federal judge will be assigned to hear the appeal and is granted broad latitude in working with the parties. It is common for the federal judge to conduct a preliminary meeting with the parties and their attorneys in an attempt to understand the issues. Often the federal judge will refer the parties to another judge, called a magistrate, who will act as a mediator in an attempt to resolve the issues without a formal hearing. If the magistrate is unsuccessful in obtaining a settlement, the parties will move on to a formal appeal. During the appeal process, the federal judge will review the hearing officer's decision and will, in most cases, give it some weight or influence. The parties will present their rationale for their appeal, introduce any new evidence to support their case, and the judge will, in a few months, render a decision on the appeal. The federal judge will either uphold the hearing decision or overturn it. The district court decision can be appealed to a federal circuit court panel for review, and after that, to the U.S. Supreme Court. (34 CFR 300.512-514)

Chapter 14

What Is My Role as a Witness in a Due Process Hearing?

The Short Answer

If you are asked to be a witness in a special education due process hearing, you will be called as a school district witness to provide information based upon your work with the special education student who is the subject of the hearing. Your testimony helps the administrative hearing officer determine the facts of the case and make a decision on the dispute. (34 CFR 300.509)

Preparing for a Hearing

A special education due process hearing is a significant undertaking that has the potential to have an adverse programmatic and fiscal impact if the district loses. Therefore, the school district should allocate sufficient time to review documents, prepare witnesses, plan effective arguments for the district's actions, and develop a compelling rebuttal to allegations made by the parent's attorney.

To prepare yourself for testifying in a due process hearing, you should carefully review all of the relevant documents in the case. Some of the documents you have developed, such as notes to the parent or an activity log; others you already have seen, such as the IEP or assessment reports. You should be comfortable and familiar with all of the documents that will be introduced into evidence and linked to your testimony. Your credibility as a witness depends upon your ability to answer questions regarding the written documents with confidence and authority.

In addition to reviewing the documents, you should understand the issues that have led to the hearing and the parent's allegations. As a witness, you should be prepared to respond to questions regarding your work with the student. The school district's attorney will ask you questions during direct testimony, and it is likely the parent's attorney will cross-examine you. Your pre-hearing interviews with the school district's attorney and the district's special education administrator will help you become comfortable with the questions asked by both sides.

Testifying in the Hearing

Your testimony will be scheduled for a certain day and an approximate time. Since it's difficult to predict exactly when you will be called to testify, you should plan to arrive early in case you are called sooner than expected. You will wait outside the hearing room because you are not permitted to listen to the testimony of other witnesses. When you are called, the hearing officer will swear you in and your testimony will begin.

The school district's attorney will lead you through your testimony by posing a series of questions. The questions you will be asked are questions you have reviewed with the school district's attorney in your pre-hearing meetings. The sequence of questions will typically begin with your educational background, including your degrees, major field of study, credentials or certification, and current assignment. Once these preliminaries are completed, you will be asked questions about your relationship and knowledge of the student, eventually leading to questions that are directly linked to the disputed issues. During your testimony, the school district's attorney will direct your attention to any documents that are linked to your testimony and may ask additional questions to clarify any issues that need emphasis.

When you have completed your direct testimony, you will be cross-examined by the parent's attorney. In addition to asking you questions about your responses during direct testimony, the parent's attorney may ask other questions regarding your involvement with the student that go beyond your direct testimony. At the conclusion of the cross-examination, the hearing officer may pose a question or two before you are excused. In most cases, once you are excused you are finished as a witness, but sometimes you can be recalled if either attorney wishes to ask additional questions.

How to Be a Good Witness

You are being asked to testify in a due process hearing because you have information that is helpful to the school district's presentation to the hearing officer. To be a good witness, you need to respond to questions in a clear and convincing manner.

When you are asked a question, make sure that you fully understand the question you are being asked. Sometimes a witness is uncertain of the question, but doesn't want to appear unprepared or unintelligent and answers anyway. If you are uncertain of the question, it's fine to ask for a restatement of the question if you're not sure about what's being requested.

You may be asked a question you don't know the answer to, and it's okay to state that you don't know. Some witnesses may resist admitting they don't know something they think they "should" know, but if you don't have the information requested, it's better to say so.

You should be careful to only answer the question that you are asked and not "volunteer" more information. It's important to listen carefully to the question and focus your response directly to the point of the question. Do not read into a question more than is intended and resist the temptation to embellish upon a response. If the attorney has the need for more information, she will always pose a follow-up question.

You may be asked questions that may be provocative or upsetting, but you should remain calm and keep your feelings in check. You are a trained and competent professional and shouldn't respond to a hostile question as a personal attack. Your effectiveness as a witness will be based, in part, upon your ability to maintain your credibility and composure, even under the trying circumstances of a due process hearing.

Chapter 15

What Is My Legal Liability in Special Education?

The Short Answer

As a general educator employed by a school district, you have very limited liability exposure in special education, so long as you perform the duties assigned to you in a legal and appropriate manner. If, however, you deliberately violate the law and defy school district policy and procedure, you could be subject to disciplinary action, up to and including dismissal. You also can face criminal charges and civil lawsuits that could result in personal liability exposure.

Allegations of Noncompliance and Denial of FAPE

If a special education student is enrolled in your classroom, you are required to implement all portions of the student's individualized education program (IEP) that apply to your general education class. Accommodations, modifications, behavior intervention plans, and supplementary aids and services are examples of IEP items that you may be required to address in your classroom. If you do not implement the IEP as written, the parent may file a complaint with the state department of education, alleging noncompliance with the IEP. The parent also may request a due process hearing on the issue of a denial of FAPE. An allegation of noncompliance will trigger an inquiry from the state department of education and may lead to an investigation. Typically, when a school district is found in noncompliance with an IEP, the district develops a corrective action plan, and the matter is resolved. If the parent requests a due process hearing, one will be held to determine if the district did, in fact, fail to implement the agreed-upon IEP and denied the special education student the entitlement to a "free, appropriate public education." If the hearing officer decides that the school district denied the student FAPE, the district will be required to implement the IEP as written, pay attorney's fees and other costs the parent may have incurred and may be required to pay the cost of compensatory services. (34 CFR 300.507-513, 34 CFR 300.660-662)

Allegations of noncompliance and denial of FAPE usually do not result in any liability exposure for you as the general educator, unless it can be proven that you refused to implement the IEP and the parent files a civil suit against you. If it is proven that you refused to implement the IEP of a special education student assigned to your class, the court could award monetary damages and you could be held liable for that judgment.

Allegations of Negligence

In some cases, parents of students with disabilities have attempted to sue school districts because their child did not make academic progress. Under the IDEA, the IEP does not constitute a guarantee that the student will meet his goals or make the anticipated academic progress, but merely that the school district will make a good-faith effort to implement the IEP. If, as a general educator, you can demonstrate that you have attempted to implement the IEP as written, you cannot be held liable if the student fails to meet goals or make academic progress. If, however, you did not attempt to implement the IEP as written and could not perform your assigned duties because you were under the influence of alcohol or drugs, you may be found to be negligent and could be subject to disciplinary action, criminal charges and civil lawsuits.

Allegations of Discrimination and Harassment

Special education students are protected from discrimination and harassment based upon their disabilities under Section 504 of the Rehabilitation Act, a federal law prohibiting discrimination and harassment. Under Section 504 requirements, school districts are required to adopt policies and procedures that protect students and staff from discrimination and harassment based upon factors such as race, religion, ethnicity, gender, age and disability. If there is an allegation of discrimination under Section 504, the federal Office for Civil Rights (OCR) will conduct an investigation. If the investigation findings determine that the allegation is valid, the school district will be required to develop a corrective action plan that is approved by the

OCR to resolve the compliant. If, in the course of the investigation, the Office for Civil Rights finds that you, in your capacity as a general educator, did deliberately discriminate or harass the special education student assigned to your classroom, you may be subject to disciplinary action and, if the parent files a civil suit against you and prevails, monetary damages. (Rehabilitation Act of 1973, 29 USC Sections 706(8), 794, 794a, 794b; 34 CFR Part 104; 42 USC 12132; 28 CFR Part 35; U.S. Department of Education Letter of July 25, 2000)

Avoiding Personal Liability

Your best protection against personal liability exposure is to follow the requirements of the students' IEPs that apply to your classroom and to maintain a learning environment that is free from discrimination and harassment. Your professionalism and commitment to perform your duties in compliance with all legal requirements, district policies and procedures will enable you to avoid any personal liability in special education.